BABY'S FIRST VALENTINE

© CATHERINE HABBIE

Prologue

Baby spends the first Valentine's Day pondering over the strange behaviour of the world around her. Right before her eyes, red hearts pop out everywhere, in all shapes and sizes. She really cannot figure out why.

Walk along with baby as the madness of Valentine's Day is revealed through baby's eyes.

There are hearts in shops everywhere.

Big red ones and little pink ones too!

Sounds like a recipe for global heartache.

When shops sell heart-shaped balloons, chocolates and even cake.

Flower shops selling a bouquet of 100 or a single, red-stemmed rose. Oh, I don't understand why anyone would need those!

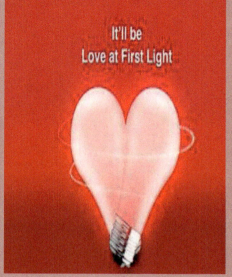

Everyone is talking about Valentine's Day. In the ads on the telly all day.

FEBRUARY

Sunday	Monday	Tuesday	Wednesday	Thursday	Friday	Saturday
					1	2
3	4	5	6	7	8	9
10	11	12	13	14	15	16
17	18	19	20	21	22	23
24	25	26	27	28		

Mum reminds Dad all the time. He has even marked the day on his calendar lest he forget like last time.

This sounds scary, even my sister gets teary. I know Valentine's Day is on 14th February.

What is this day all about? History says it was Saint Valentine who helped lovers a lot.

Hmmm... I wonder who'll be mine?

I've only ever had a solitary play date with a baby! It doesn't really matter; I don't have the time.

My sister says I need to grow up first. I'm just too young to be bothered by this love outburst.

I drift off to sleep gazing at the heart-shaped world outside my crib. Few dry tears that I wipe on my bib.

The sun rose the next morning, and it wasn't pink. The birds chirped and it wasn't red. It was Valentine's Day, and I was still in bed.

I heard dad marching 'noiselessly' up the stairs. He's made enough noises to wake up bears.

My sister is already on the phone, I hope today will not make her moan.

I guess it'll just be me and the nice baby-sitter. She is always sweet and never bitter.

I scratch my baby curls and suck my thumb, prepared for an interesting day with humans acting dumb.

Wait I hear footsteps, someone is coming to my crib. 'Good morning sunshine' says mum.

She's brought me a card, what fun! 'With all my love' she says, and I know it's no fib.

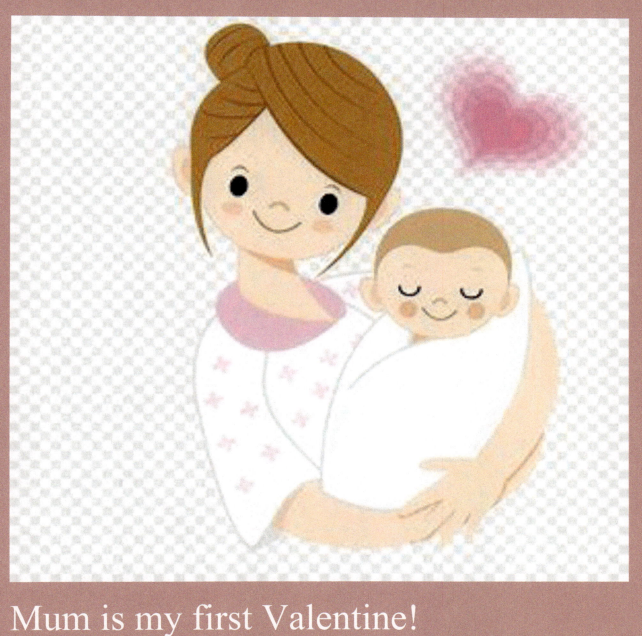

Mum is my first Valentine!

She hugs and kisses me on my cheeks. I'll certainly be good for the next few weeks.

I cannot wait to eat the yummy chocolates when I have some teeth. Hope you have a Valentine's Day that is just as sweet.

THE END

THE HISTORY OF

VALENTINES DAY

Valentine's Day, also called Saint Valentine's Day or the Feast of Saint Valentine, is celebrated annually on February 14.[2] It originated as a Christian feast day honouring a martyr named Valentine, and through later folk traditions it has also become a significant cultural, religious and commercial celebration of romance and love in many regions of the world.

There are a number of martyr-dom stories associated with various Saint Valentines connected to February 14, including an account of the imprisonment of Saint Valentine of Rome for ministering to Christians persecuted under the Roman Empire in the third century.

According to an early tradition, Saint Valentine restored sight to the blind daughter of his jailer.

Numerous later additions to the legend have better related it to the theme of love: tradition maintains that Saint Valentine performed weddings for Christian soldiers who were forbidden to marry by the Roman emperor; an 18th-century embellishment to the legend claims he wrote the jailer's daughter a letter signed "Your Valentine" as a farewell before his execution.

The 8th-century recorded the celebration of the Feast of Saint Valentine on February 14.

The day became associated with romantic love in the 14th and 15th centuries, when notions of courtly love flourished, apparently by association with the "lovebirds" of early spring.

In 18th-century England, it grew into an occasion for couples to express their love for each other by presenting flowers, offering confectionery, and sending greeting cards (known as "valentines").

Valentine's Day symbols that are used today include the heart-shaped outline, doves, and the figure of the winged Cupid.

In the 19th century, handmade cards gave way to mass-produced greetings.

In Italy, Saint Valentine's keys are given to lovers "as a romantic symbol and an invitation to unlock the giver's heart", as well as to children to ward off epilepsy (called Saint Valentine's Malady).

Valentine's Day is not a public holiday in any country.

Books by Catherine Habbie

Baby Goes to London

Baby Loves Baking

Baby in the Garden

Baby Goes to School

Baby & New Baby

Baby Goes to Space

Baby's First Easter

Baby's First Christmas

Baby's First Halloween

Baby in the Orchard

Baby in the Vegetable Patch

Baby in Lockdown

Printed in Great Britain
by Amazon